Carol and Ahoy

By the same author:

Poetry
First Names
The Yellow Gum's Conversion
The Ladder

Non-fiction
The Selected Poetry of Guido Cavalcanti
Dear Muses? Essays on Poetry

Carol and Ahoy

Simon West

PUNCHER & WATTMANN

First published in 2018
Published by Puncher and Wattmann
PO Box 279
Waratah NSW 2298

http://www.puncherandwattmann.com

puncherandwattmann@bigpond.com

A catalogue record for this
book is available from the
National Library of Australia

ISBN   9781925780109

Cover design by Miranda Douglas

Printed by Lightning Source International

This project has been assisted by the Australian Government through the Australia Council, its arts funding and advisory body.

Australian Government

Australia Council
for the Arts

in memoriam

D. W. W.

Contents

River Tracks

Never a straight line or a single course,
never blue. Most maps mistell you.
Eager to find where you finish,
they mistake your daydreaming, your loops
and faux pas and odd sidesteps,
your misgivings and floods of largesse.

Round Murchison it's said the Ngooraialum
called you Bayungun, but Mitchell
might have got this wrong. Waaring
was also recorded, while downstream you were Kialla
and Goopna, deep waterhole,
living on in Congupna and Tallygaroopna.
Tongue sounds taken for runs, then stations
and finally the towns that drank you –
black names that gave white settlers licence to the land.
Your big-picture title, Goulburn, was something new.
More skittish than Proteus, all water's ancestor,
you've flowed through many guises, your track
was spun to unravel without end.
Was it merely a twist of fate
that one of your Yorta Yorta names was Moira?

Rarely have you had to hop, skip and jump
through drought like your cousin the Broken.
From the up-high of satellite and migrating bird,
who know their course by impulse,
you're as unkempt as a camper's hair,
as fickle and fractious as a child,

you're running hands-first through the dark,
going the long way to the sea.

Round Shepp I walk a tract of park
scooped by your failed forays, trenches
greedy with grass and frog croaks.
Some open to billabongs, those castaways
that await like long-suffering red gums
your next incursion and siege. They dream
of a time when you rise to conquer clay
baked hard and fissured and tinder raw,
when you release each rut of old snags
and your salve spreads like a truce
submerging paddocks and fences,
licking at roads and property,
letting us bide for a bit in common reflection.

Hans Heysen

The difficulty in mist-thick light
was to keep the gum tree solid. Its trunk
moves to the top of the frame just like
an obelisk in fog. Like a mother
it holds in the sway of its skirts the lie
of the land to the thumb-tall hills, a litter
of leaves and a passing child; and draws the sky
down from a peak to steep it in the picture.

The difficulty was to keep its bulk
where light-coloured trunk and limbs were seen
against the sun's raw morning bulb,
to paint the wooded weight of tree,
with its sap and slant and stubborn hold,
yet show light playing through the leaves,
as truth, world's truth, not absolute, is blent
and filters through our pulsing temperament.

On a Trip to Van Diemen's Land

Walking above a bluestone bridge I tilt
against the rails. I watch its trickling stream
trying to conjure sentenced men who built
this crossing and set my stage — mid-nineteenth-
century men, hardened by exile till
they shed the burden home set on their dreams:
my ancestors, my house whose memory
is stunted like the broken bole of a tree.

On my mother's side, out from County Clare
came Ellen Smith — illiterate, eyes green,
a widowed dairymaid who stole a cow,
complexion pale, one child in charge, RC.
She wed, in Hobart, Aaron Hibbard, collier,
head small, complexion swarthy, C. of E.
Whether their lives blazed or were cold as slate
the only records now are those of State.

I kindle names with facts, or chart
a distant origin: from York, Carlisle,
Northumberland and Kent. Places I'd learnt
in Shakespeare's worlds, swapped for this sceptred isle
where outcasts nursed the wounds an Empire's blunt
blade dug in a demi-paradise
of postcard pastures with their docile game,
a wound that festered past the change of name.

Death wiped a shipwrecked generation's slate.
Their children seemed to spring from wind-tossed seed
and grew staked to the mores of English State.
My grandmother denied her convict breed,
kept corgies, never uttered words like *mate*.
She found no cause to doubt the proper creeds
or think Fitzgerald's might be built on sand.
One never dwelt on tribes who'd lost their land.

The stream below says make your ancestors.
Choose that wild goose John Boyle O'Reilly, shipped
to a land of Oyster-and-Ale. Take poets who sought
to shape examined lives in song. Their gifts
are prayer and tribute, just as, fleeing Troy,
Aeneas shouldered father, son and Lares.
And before your own transport to fog-thick seas
cling to the past and sing its legacies.

Floodplains on the Broken River

We dwelt across from bushlands where the Broken
brought the town to a halt.
As far as Mooroopna
old red gums filled the floodplains
and farming yielded to a stand of bush.
Beyond the line of bitumen
I trod on litterfall and felt under foot
a stir of living things.

I loved how that motley of leaves had laid unswept
back to the last long-distant floods,
how it accrued with sticks
and strips of bark, and bullet-hard gum nuts,
and dead grass and new growth,
and how when the river shrank
there was the reek of mud, while heat released
the scents and saps that linger in matter.

Bush-ground was time-heavy and intricate,
steeped in the elements, layered like an archeological dig.
My stance felt fortified and buoyed by earth,
but heedful, too, in long grass
and log's shadow,
of snakes and things the mind
made up, seconding a sense of trespass
over uncleared land.

In town the bush meant things best kept at bay.
You'd find dumped rubbish on its brink, while deeper in
there were signs of sculled alcohol
and furtive smokes. Once as a kid,
stooping there, I saw,
water-damaged and stiff with mud,
pages torn from a magazine. When I straightened
my heart raced to handle something so illicit.

I cast around to see if I was seen.
The challenge from the woods
wasn't for some taboo transgressed.
It was having slighted
where I stood. And now I saw each tree
rear upwards from the scrub,
like monoliths that set their timeless shape
against a restless world.

Sometimes I've sought these countries for the gleam
when, after rain or in a raking light,
having shed rough bark,
the gums stand in their tender under-skins
streaked like boiled sweets.
I bow to pick a handful of foliage –
rigid and brittle now, but still with a faint
smell of eucalyptus oil as I crush them.

Uncanny Nature

I envy the artist who with a handful of brushstrokes
captured a swallow in flight, or whose cataract,
depicted on the palace wall,
disturbed the sleep of an emperor.
What a poem distils it must also set free.
Its phrases shimmer like a sequinned dress.
Dante it seems was right: the beauty of words
adorns, enchanting our gaze. Not all is laid bare.
And thus, when a beam of sunlight prods the city at dawn,
colouring cumuli in greys and pinks,
who am I to dismiss the unworldly
or a certain sense of hope?

On Looking into a Chinese Scroll

Eddying round this unreeled scene, my eye
swims to a mountain tip then sweeps beside
the stream-washed pebbles of a valley floor.
I watch on their winding paths horsemen and porters
echo the trees that cluster on a ridge.
Perhaps those travellers on the railless bridge
will reach by night the well-tilled field and hut
that sit below the pass. Perhaps they'll halt
and see beyond inked walls of rock the house-lit
plains, or mark the petalled boughs.
I marvel how an artist proofed his scroll
by trusting to a half-glimpsed common soul.

What's soul but all we briefly hold in trust –
language and the emblems that endow a tree,
the hankering after order Plato felt,
maestà, mandala, echoes in the shell,
the signs those mountain-climbing prophets sought?
Why not evoke such words – too coy? In awe
of ... what? The rallied cries, the loose riposte?
The earth's at change – rises, falls. Is lost?
Like breath, it's soul flows through us, grounds our feet,
might be the springing point from which to reach
beyond ourselves. Unwind the scroll and cast
your eye and wonder how to give the heart,
that beats now in its scaffolding of bone,
the steadiness this artist's brush gave stone.

A Monologue on the Soul and Body

Now let the mind surrender
to the wisdom of the heart.
Cut loose each thread of thought
and wallow in the breath.
Old prophets always start
their hill-climbs from the base.
Lovers seek truth in the face.

The body knows. Both blood
and spirits are eloquent.
Soul is no hostage – feeler
by feeler the crown extends,
its purchase is the trunk.
Head's lift and soul's thin thew
Antaeus took from the root.

Waking on a Summer Morning

I asked if verse were no more than a toy,
then heard the blackbird's carol and ahoy
and the traffic's tidal snare drum sough.
They were absolute, these tones, not thought's forgotten setting now,
as they washed through open windows and the new-found
arch of door jambs, and echoed round
the room's old school of shadows. They were glory
of music on the mind's cool parquet floor.

The Turtles and the Waterfall – A Dream

I stand outside the house. I have returned
to meditate on what still fosters me,
fosters the branching mind that learns
by hunch – shapes sprung from arcane fantasies
and emblems of delight, like crossroad herms
that bide the wind's fresh voice of rivalry
and lure us with the thought of fuller lives.
Yet what the mirror shows me I despise.

Old friends arrive and crowd the lawn. We need
more chairs. I search beside the shuttered house,
where we had stacks of chairs last week,
lent for my father's wake. But now the grounds
are wide with stands of giant oaks in leaf,
torsos and pockmarked plinths. I stop to mount
a toppled column whose flutes gleam with rain.
And every chair I find has a broken frame.

I wander and my wandering is a key,
until I think my friends have been ignored.
I turn but turning see a cairn
and at its peak a spout whose water pours
into a pool. Here turtles wait to climb
the waterfall, rock climbing to its source.
And I, a childlike man of forty-five,
clutch at this vision, enchanted, terrified.

And now I'm standing in that square in Rome
where four bronze turtles scale the fountain rim,
stubborn as salmon to get home.
Why must they reach the higher basin's brim —
the current's path is easy and here below
the water dances and invites us in?
But there the four long-limbed ephebes keep
a timeless eye on time and never sleep.

Back at the Broken River

I've often sat on these banks and let the eye
float in the bush on the far side of the water.
About this anabranch, where it nudges through
the catch-all of a gully, there are annals of scrub
bordering the slop of sea-sized fields.
I imagine the box and river gums that form this brake
as a rabbled home guard
hanging on to old orders of shade.
I've wanted to find some rare word like *bosk* to name it,
but sitting here again I'm overwhelmed
by the measureless convolution of matter,
the ramifications of complex things as weird
and vast as a vista of mountains.
I take up a stick and pit holes in the dirt
and dig till the rhythm of gesture calms my thoughts
and I drift on the breath's steady course
that tugs the mind as a current does when you immerse a hand.

And now, gazing once more across the water,
I follow the living forms of things with childish awe.
In growth and decay there are such varied colours
you can hardly know them more than a marvellous dream
that fades to a muddle of browns and greens.
It's like getting lost in the count of rings on a sawn red gum.
And then how good it is to notice
what is tactile and particular.
Taking a leaf I trace the veins that pattern
its lobular form with a finger, as if intent
on a botanical drawing. Pausing
to give each cherished thing its name, I find
a poise that redeems my distance from the world.

The Limits of Parable

(Edward M. Curr — Tongala, July 1841)

When I heard them cooee from the far bank, I thought of high-blooded
Hermes on an outmission, his staff prodding the mud,

a tinkle of coins in his pouch, eager to be back among signs of order.
So far inland, who else would patrol a fitful river like a border.

My Tasmanians, where they worked at a sapling,
lowered rope and axe

and straightened stiffly. *Sir, for Christ's sake now, they're not
to be trusted. Let's kid them over and shoot the skeary lot.*

Three natives, erect as reeds, stood among
the crooked boles of river gum.

Do not our inclinations tell us this world is ours
if only we can covet it with pure hearts?

Despite not having English they implied
they would cross to speak with us if we so desired,

and in half an hour with no more than a tomahawk
they had hewn and shaped a sheet of bark. I saw

them launch from a snag that jutted like a jetty.
The water there was wide and flowed freely

but they rocked into the current without hesitation, cupped hands
for a paddle, and steered towards a sandbar

where lately we had led the thirsty sheep.
As they stood at ease by our fire, and dried their feet,

my men were once more at the edge of our newly-chosen plain
felling timber with which to contain

the livestock in a rough and ready bough yard. The crash
and devastation and each novel sign of our sudden possession

attracted the attention of my sable guests. And yet
no word of surprise escaped them. Were they not

in their detachment like children
of the woods, who still must learn

we will never enjoy the world aright
until we seize God's talent to give back multiplied?

Yore

A dove whose two notes wake you at first light.
A tidal stream we wade in day by day.
A balm, an itch, a presence hard to touch.
The haze of stars we call the milky way.
A market stall wrapped up in tarps at night.

A tongue's tip which has lost the words to dart.
A road that's growing darker at your back.
A snowcapped cliff that holds us in its shade.
The longing of a lover. Rome to sack.
A pond. A poem you once knew by heart.

Turned loam where withered bulbs send up new shoots.
A bed of reeds just as a duck flies out.
A rut. A slate wiped clean but hastily.
A box, a book, a magician's empty hat.
The house you dwell in with its thousand rooms.

On Reading Again of David and Goliath

At last I've looked up *cuirass*.
I'm not meticulous enough with language.
I'd always pictured David
stepping out from ranks with just his sling
I hardly saw what he had spurned. Some nouns
met in dateless stories hold their peace.
Eager to get on we gloss over them.
Goliath is waiting. Two armies catch their breath.
Besides, we're told reality is not precise.

But now I am glad to have found this garb.
Words too must face the world, and need defence.
Despite all laws of likelihood, may leaps
of faith restore their brilliance to our lives.
Let's call them clothing for mind's nakedness.

Psalm

Our awe clinics? They're outsourced now.
It's a thin but efficient reality.
From where will it come the epiphany fix,
the peek at the sacred now?
On Sabbath days,
on loose fairweather days
we hit the paths of bitumen,
we flee suburbs that repeat
like rippled water round a vanished stone.
We race on past upsized paddocks,
marking skylines flung far off like something primordial,
we bob across the undulant terrain
until within whiff of our end
and turning off highways
we gully down humbler approaches,
slowing in awkward deference now
where dancing ground spits pebbles and a wake of dust
to coat the unfenced crowds of bush.

And here's our harbour,
a clearing in the tree muster,
a welcome lack from which to watch
this new-found much-ado community,
all the more imposing as each trunk
soars with wide-limbed ease
out of the teem of immanence.

We lull in this place,
the lost-gaze spot,
the bellbird-charted dome,

settling on unfurled rugs while children
paddle barefoot across the grass.
And who are these that come now,
sweeping gravity in their wake
at Grant's picnic ground?
The stained-glass-coloured birds,
the cocky-voiced birds,
descending to feed off open palms,
the eager avian angels.

We self-bestow the stout-soled boots
to follow the curves of forest track
into the scrub moil,
the fuss of fallen foliage,
in search of wilder Edens.
We seek round Lederderg
in the smooth-worn rocks of a waterfall,
or down Gippsland way in a grove
of Gondwanan beeches,
or over in Gariwerd in the smell
of a cave that's safekept images for chiliads.

What are we with our thoughts,
what's this twilight fidgeting
and ordering of the elements?
And there in the rhythm of your own footfalls,
feet walking in a world too big for them by far,
and you glad of it,
in a world uncut to size, reality is rich
like sunlit water that takes on the tannins of tea trees,
and that swirl of eternity set in our hearts is calm now,
and we lie down in peace and sleep now.

Agave on the Victorian Coast

There's something worthy here, something to wonder at.
So you stop on your walk to watch
from the tower's squint-defences, the light-shy fissures,
seeking the underside of foliage, the shadow-bellies of canopy.
In the dry heat, in the cicada surge of noon.
Eardrums taut as a beaten calfskin throb with sluggish blood,
the mind-lulling Bacchic blood,
limb-loosening heat of laconics and oracles
in which one ringing word quickens like a quake: Agave.
And in the undergrowth's kindling blanket, fodder-level set for a fire,
there's a flit of colour between two banksia trunks,
so your mind's eye sweeps the inner room, the ever-attended hearth,
and thinks – why not? – of Maenads.
A Maenad's no wilder than the seeds of this Jurassic plant
and transports well as this stoic cliff-gripping sentinel
who once marked oared warships over the Aegean
and still stores manna in Mexican deserts.

You stare at the scabs of light off Bass Strait,
each weightless scale that dazzles like mica stars in bitumen,
and you long to scoop that silver pond scum off and from this height
to drop into liquid. It would be like plunging yourself
through a mirror's frenzied atoms
to a dimension of fathoms that suck out air and, more gradually, light.
It would be to dissipate like a clump of humid salt
and undo and ingod yourself and know for certain or not.
It would be, but for the holding back, the not that recalls
the stubborn tooth-lined tongues of the agave.
Panting leathery leaves. With length they collapse on themselves.
Then their tips are dipping swan beaks or the blind

snubs of dolphins, a mute drooping
that butts the waterless ground.
And yet, how each leaf serves to give shape, to clear a way
for the rosetta's core, the real explosion, the monocarpic esse
more replete and patient than most lifetimes,
flower that sways like a crow's nest
crowning the top of a self-hoisted mast,
lookout longing for something more,
cupola where the wasps come seeking sweetness.

You watch from the shade and wonder.
You watch and call yourself Pentheus.
You watch and loosen your rhythms.
You watch but summoned words just bend and shed
like water off the back of aqua suede, the bending leggings
of the agave. You step out in the heat to test those teeth
against the flick of your nail. You tap the cartilaginous stem,
squinting in the fierce light. Light to tear one apart.
You open your mouth to give voice
and utter a guttural hum, a digging-in of sound,
comforting the heart and the belly,
like the purr of the seeking bee, the seeker of song.

The Lorikeets

All morning since dawn they have come,
this band of parrots, to feed on our flowering gum.
Their volleys of noise
are deafening. I get dizzy
trying to hold one voice as it mounts
then is lost to like cries, rapid
as automatic gunfire.
There's something frantic about their assembly,
so I see men
slowly submerged and fierce at the cost of mates
to be saved from fathomless water.

At first in the canopy
the parrots are camouflaged, so I think
perhaps the trunk itself holds souls
who plead for release. But then you see
a flash of purple or bright yellow –
the underwing of the lorikeet –
as they dart away or return in small sorties,
or you see one swing from a yielding twig,
and it's then you grasp
how the whole head
is animate with clambering birds,
all of them eager to assert
brief rights to each new inflorescence.

Why can't I yoke this flock's loud feasting song
to a sense of joy, and pretend I too belong?
Their being in league makes me think
of pitting oneself, a brazen

headrush that smothers compassion
and lets us forget the unbreathable depths of space.
And I remember once when as kids our gang
seized on a scapegoat – one of our own –
and taunted him. I drew back
from the same frenzied chant
as voices detached from the sense of words
and became another kind of energy.

There is so much clamour I wonder
if perhaps they are drunk. In a craze
they tear each bud to free the cream-white stamens,
then plunge their tongues after nectar
whose smell is pungent as privet flowers.
By midmorning the bacchanal is over.
When I walk out the ground is strewn with little round caps
like a rout of shields after an Athenian battle.
At dusk they'll return at the urge of their guts
to gorge on the bounty of some nameless god.
For a spell they'll be invincible, and their rites
will mock the heavens for losing hold of the light.

Boundary Line

I stopped to watch some schoolboys playing cricket.
Across the outfield to the oval's edge
the coos of players round the wicket
travelled faint as the cries of high migrating birds.
It was that moment of hiatus, batsmen
prodding the turf, while fielders, set at ease,
held then tossed the dead ball in a chain
back to the bowler, each one eager to test
the leather like a charm and know its weight.
I love that instant when the bowler starts his run.
The batsman with his bat just off the ground
is spellbound till the ball is loosed and scuds
towards his stumps. In a flash he must attack
or let it pass. Then there's another lull
till slowly everything is set again.

Above that stretch of open city ground
the autumn sky sat vast and still. I noticed
how its colour changed from something pale
and see-through, where it met the gaze,
to a lush uncanny depth beyond my head.
Up there this ball must seem a speck
of red that's moved around a ring of grass
which kids have hallowed through their game,
as if these rules were a kind of ritual
and for a spell the boundary line
might keep the motion of the world at bay.

I recalled a teacher once from years ago
whose voice still pitches in my head as he tackled
a despondency I'd bared, *Come on, what's wrong?*
It's these should be the best days of your life.
More bitter than befriending, his urgency
startled me into a begrudged retreat.
I have sought my own hard way to faith in things.
But as if he lingered now for my forgiveness
I felt at last the weight of what he meant,
the stone-like onus of watching from a tangent,
toeing the rim of a field, wistful for something
lost or passed on one day unwillingly.

Walking in the Bush at Whroo

As I walked in the scrub
and ironbarks at Whroo
I listened to the cicadas
that sang in the heat of noon.
I'd dwelt with downcast mind
on the movements of the day
with their cocksure bullying cries
until I had nothing to say.
I had weighed hope with the shafts
old pitmen dug in these grounds
for dreamt-up veins of gold
drought nudged them to renounce.
It's dry, black-trunked country.
Plenty perished without fruits.
It's hard to carry a name
while living on trimmed roots.
Half lost in litterfall
are shin-high stakes that mark
fools who shadowed gold
under the ironbarks.

That music will rally a mind
like headwinds off a coast
whose primal notes are crude
and cold as an ocean's boast.
But I listened and it seemed
those insects from the stones
were driven by a need
to avow old love with their own,
to fathom a dying branch

and the eggs left as a gift,
the spider-like nymphs that fell
to a course of katabasis
where, fostered by black roots,
the imago grew well-fed
as the living learn to bear
visions left by the dead.
On warm nights after rain
like miners in reverse
they'd butt the sticky soil
to claim a second birth.

I saw that moment a seam
splits their earthy shell
and having climbed the tree
they climb out of themselves
and unfurl a filigree
of wings like glistening fronds
and their tymbals begin to pulse
and then burst with beholden song.
I walked alone in that bush
and heard the cicadas' peal.
Had something changed? Well no.
But I stood in a world that was real.

After Looking at Donatello's Reliefs for the Pulpit of Prato

I once thought ardour of the mind
was proof that pride was justified.
I trusted more in words and forms
than in the light-struck cumuli.
Things of the earth transform.

Why heed the bell tower, why think twice
when reason falters at a rhyme?
Passing, why touch a pitted herm
or step into an empty shrine?
Things of the earth transform.

And now these putti dance and laugh
and catch each turning of the heart,
raising their timbrels and their horns.
What can we still expect of art?
Things of the earth transform.

How Else?

If I ever reach the capital's high walls
and, having gained admittance through the gates
adorned with the emblems of fallen
provinces, I climb the winding street
and flagstoned stairs to where,
beneath a trellised vine just off the square,
the Duke's courtiers sit at ease,
one of whom turns to ask with a laugh,
what is poetry?, and the conversation, which has raced
with many voices like a spring stream, lulls,
and each expectant face settles on me,
then I shall have my answer ready.

For as I walked out this morning I saw
a flock of ibis cross the clouds of dawn.
I heard their faint cries. The air was crisp
and in the distance
mountains trembled like a scrap of cloth.
My senses rallied to the scene, yet I clutched
at words like driftwood tossed on the sea.
How else can we suggest such complexity
or recall our longing the way a boy once watched
slow-moving birds cross his valley and thought
of the city whose shopfronts and billboards
were decorated with so many bold-faced words?

A Twenty-First-Century Poet Timidly Addresses the Muse

Dear Muse, I know a man who has vowed to wink
whenever he invokes you. His poems gauge
the tightness of the lips that make a smile
hover between a sneer and dispassionate play.
Some have played the role of Socrates
so well their wit has hardened into zeal.
Although they have demeaned their enemies
the price is our shared vision of what's real.
I don't know if you wear a swimming costume,
flaunting your features and eternal youth,
or, dressed in a stola, you control the tribune,
or yearn like the Sibyl in her cave for death.
Rather I think of world-old anima mundi,
and know where I find my words in unison
it was miracle not acumen of mine
that took the lead, some timely intuition
that cuts across the nihilistic bars
we hold before the world. I think of how
you sanction song that calls the moon and stars.
Stand by me, Muse. Without you we would howl.

How it Should Be

'I spent my life composing rhythmical spells'

— Czesław Miłosz

Well perhaps, but what you left
weren't pretty stars sent out to graze the sky,
or gibbering rhymes repeated in the dead of night.
I think of canny prayers and cautious flashes
where a current jumped between two fervent words.
I think of a child conversing with an imaginary friend,
or imagination *hovering between images*.
That's Coleridge. He shared your avid
wonder at the beauty of the world.
You kept its forms alive in reasoned spells.

The Magic Box – Nonna Tells a Fairy Tale

Casale Monferrato June 2015

I see in the unlit room our shadowed forms
against the evening light the windows frame.
Above the courtyard and pent fields of corn
swallows avow new claims and counterclaims.
And then, Nonna, what happens next? Go on!
You tug back through the press of time a tale.
First witness to this summoned world, heeding
your braid of words, my daughter stands by your knee.

You tell of Fortune's hand in human things,
that fickle wheel that jerks from old
disharmonies to new, new rules that ring
like knells for those downcast, then of a box,
a magic box from which a feast could spring,
of debt undone, a father helped then fooled,
wild journeys through a wood, a witch who smiled,
of devils and the quick wits of a child.

I marvel how this long-pooled fable rises
from the unforced grounds of memory, how it draws
back to the surface your deep-held delight
when forebears shared their eagerness for lore.
I think how words can eddy privately
and waste a common gift in weltered thoughts
that chart our ebb from bitterness to death
or grieve to ghosts we call as audience.

May we recall tonight, this tale, its telling.
It can't be fastened on the page. It idles
in potentia, wells by chance, when met
it's like it was always known by heart, like vital
water that can spring from stone. The present
for all its fears is porous, the past survives.
And some day may my daughter spring this box
and cast the spell that breaks time's bounding rock.

Chi a questa storia non crede ha gli occhi ma non vede.

Swimming

Too neat for ghosts the borrowed house was airless
as a scene from Ibsen.
I haunted your not being there
and counted down as currawongs glibly
heralded then mourned each day.
Late on the last wet afternoon, more
restless than convivial, I walked
towards the bay.

A clump of coastal pines,
a blanket of needles where the cliff declines
and the headland curls up to the beach.
Pitching forward I snatched at each
branch across the stepless
track. Halfway down it turns west
and falls to where the surfers launch off
cramped black rocks.
I stuck to the thicket and leant against a trunk,
whose roots I reckon would first have sunk
into the earth
about the time of your own father's birth.
Tall trees and through the tessellated boles, the sea.
I have no memory of him, just a photo with no frame.
I'm sitting loosely on his knee.
You never spoke of him nor of his wife —
I barely knew their names —
as though the past were some grim sheet
of ocean, fathomless and without life.
On beachside holidays, a sentinel with naked feet,
you squinted at the waves, and smoothed the sand of flaws.

When I picture you with water
I see you gloved and in a greenhouse
administering each seedling its daily dose.

I stood and watched it clashing with the shore.
Elemental things – too vast, you'd say, for words, too,
                                primal and unchanged.
The mass of half-beached kelp.
The wind the terns and oystercatchers ranged.
I'd never seen this place before.
I wasn't likely to return. And yet I felt
a kind of deference.
I thought of you. The thought bridged both your being
and not being, and made no sense.
Perhaps some recognition did take place.
Perhaps my vision of you out there swimming
meant that something was restored.
I don't know what or if I'd call it grace.
Why not say I watched the tide, the dipping birds,
and felt a kind of peace?
And then I nodded to the trees and went.

The Twofold Tree

in memoriam D.W.W.

'And now, Aeneas – since your sight is bound –
know that your friend lies dead, his unmourned corpse
cast on the sand, dishonouring the fleet,
while like a child who seeks decrees you linger
round our threshold. Go. First you must bare
a mortal to his resting place and build
his tomb and with the black-skinned cattle make
your sacrifice. Otherwise forget
your wish to tread the woods of Styx,
that place kept pathless to the living.'

The sibyl stepped away into the dark.
Dispirited, Aeneas left the cave,
the sibyl's forecasts swirling through his brain.
Archates walked with him. He too was dazed
and struggled to give form to this foreboding.
But as they hurried back towards the ships
they sought hard words to share their wildest fears.
Who – which friend – lay waiting by the water?

And there cast on the shore as they appeared,
taken undeservedly to death,
Misenus, dear Misenus lay, whom none
excelled in rousing troops and stirring Mars
to combat with his trumpet's piercing cry.
Once he strode at Hector's side,
his sounded brass helped hold the standard high.
But when Achilles struck poor Hector dead
Misenus joined Aeneas and his men
to seek adventures no less grand.

Now one day as he blew a hollow shell,
delighting in its clear and booming call,
he cried a boastful challenge to the Gods,
and Triton, emulous – or so it's told –
took up the dare and swept him from the rocks
to flounder in the thrash of foaming waves.

And so Aeneas and his comrades gather
round the corpse and mourn aloud.
And in their sorrow, wary of the sibyl's
words, they hasten to build up the pyre
and vie to find the biggest logs to burn.
They rove into an ancient forest –
fit element for unknown beasts.
Their axe blows echo, pines crash to the ground,
sharp wedges split the wood of ash and oak,
and down huge slopes the massive rowans roll.

First among them, striving hard to wield
the tools and spur his comrades on, Aeneas
toiled but still his mind found ways to wander
round the boundless forest. Daunted, he prayed:
'I wish that somehow in this wilderness
that golden bough might show itself to me
since all the sibyl said of you, Misenus,
has thus unravelled into truth'.

He'd scarcely finished when two doves flew down
and landed near his feet. Aeneas laughed.
His mother, surely, sent these lucky birds.
And so he spoke to them: 'If any path
exists then lead me on to find
that precious branch that shadows fertile ground.

And you, dear goddess, mother, keep my cares
before your eye.' Aeneas paused and watched
for any sign. Then having fed, the birds
flew forth, but just so far, and he who followed
always had them in his sight. And thus
they reached Avernus with its stink of death.

Once here the two doves shot into the sky
then swooped low down, alighting on a tree,
the twofold tree – whose gold shone through the gloom.
Just as in winter woods the mistletoe
shoots forth its yellow leaves to bush about
the dark trunk of its host, so too this bough
of gold leaf rustled in the breeze like foil.
Aeneas seized the growth and tugged.
He felt it snap and then the shock
that shimmied up his arm. Quickly
he bore it to the sibyl's cave.

Meanwhile the Trojans mourned Misenus
and set to hounour him with death's last rites.
At first they piled up logs of oak and pine
to build the massive pyre. Against its side
they stacked whole cypress trees and at its top
they set his armour and the glittering shield.
Next from huge copper urns placed on the flames
they scooped out water that would cleanse the corpse.

Some wept again to lay him on the bier
and cover him in custom's purple shroud.
Then others took the bier to crown the pyre
and lit the torches with averted eyes
and watched as the fire burned through gifts of food

and frankincense, and bowls brimming with oil.
Then once the flames had lulled and wood had thinned
to ash that shivered in the breeze, they quenched
with wine the eager coals. It was Corynaeus
who now gathered the bones in a bronze urn
and taking up an olive branch walked thrice
around his comrades, sprinkling each with water
so they stood delivered of this death.
Finally he spoke the last farewell.

And now Aeneas built a stalwart tomb
that rose until it stood against the sky,
and here he set Misenus' arms of war,
his oar and trumpet too, and gave that place
his name, a name to keep forever more.

A Goulburn Valley Eclogue

Two poets are talking at Jim's place. Scott, the younger man, is a struggling dairy farmer.

Jim
And so you've sold just shy of half the herd?

Scott
Jim, it was that or beg the bank. They've said no
once already. That door's closed.
The price of milk has dropped, and just last week
the premiums for our place jumped.
There's nothing they won't flog insurance for.
They think our future's like this channelled land
to order into pastures, orchards, cows.

Jim
Scott, forget that accidental stuff.
Keep your eye on what's essential, life's ...

Scott
Don't think what blokes decide in city boardrooms
won't find a way to force your idyll.
This land's no garden of delight.
It's risk for you and those you bring along.
One poor year and you're back on credit.
Two and the bank has got you by the balls –
you're sold up, in some shit-hole in the suburbs,
consumed by pride, begrudging former mates
their safe routines and salaries.
Too distraught to tackle song.

Jim

But life's realities lie somewhere else.
They're not your midnight qualms or guilt's carping,
they're not the price of lucerne in a drought.
It's what we rarely wake to see –
this living world. Look at the way late light
sifts through that row of saplings on the bank.
Find words to sing of that in lasting form.

Scott

Easy for you, you're safe from cares.
You're all white hair meets solitude.
I haven't time to take a leak, but you,
you sprawl here in the shade your oak trees make.
Your table's full of food each arts grant buys.
You've ceded pristine farming land to bush,
and there's your token bay tree guards the house,
and literary friends on weekend getaways
who keep you stocked with gossip and good wine.

Jim

I don't deny my luck, Scott, but I'm proud
to have taken risks for what's important.
I've stayed sharp-eyed and stubborn in the face
of expectations. I've learnt to live with less.

Scott

Sometimes I think back on this place
as Curr tells it: the unmarred plains
that saved his herd of starving sheep,
the truce the Bangerang bestowed so he
could decree new runs by letter to the Club.

Jim

Curr tells it like a youthful stunt,
a game of capital meets confidence.
He never lost the compass of back home,
a State to take your winnings or stooped head.
For a lark he called his convicts Corydon,
sang how they sat *sub tegmine eucalypti.*

Scott

What right have we to sing a stolen land?
The cocksure shouts and cooees of those settlers
have given way to guilt that mutes our songs.

Jim

There was never any gift outright.
What they wrote back then, the squatters,
weren't songs so much as naming rights.

Scott

And what's been our inheritance? That world's
all dust. Under the onus of dispossessors
we're left to labour land long cleared
of scrub and timber, and broken down
by the aimless tap of cloven hooves
till topsoil dissipates like dirty smoke.
I've just been walking by the bridge, you know
that red gum with the yoni scar? Will we ever
find such strength of union with the land?

Jim

For Christ's sake are we damned to crow our songs?
Sure, pay respect to that first mob who struggle
still to keep a hold on land and language.

But don't pool in your own despair.
These twisting rivers and the towering forms
of river gums, our footfalls over ground
uneven for the accretions of the bush,
all this is in our blood. If fate
saw fit to drop us here, then who are we
to envy an idyllic ease in Wordsworth
or those Irish bards? They too had battles.
Turn contrition to some good. But look,
that storm bank in the west has caught the sun
and shadows lengthen down the plain.
Soon hail guns will fire over orchards.
Come on, let's have a drink. I've wine
and this new poem to share. Such fears
are better sung than dwelt upon.

Acknowledgements

The poem 'Hans Heysen' includes phrases reworked from Heysen's letters. 'The Limits of Parable' is written in the voice of Edward M. Curr, one of the first squatters in North-Central Victoria and author of *Recollections of Squatting in Victoria* (1883). I like to imagine that, as well as his beloved Bryon, Curr had been reading Thomas Traherne's *Centuries*, though this was not rediscovered until roughly ten years after Curr's death in 1889. The poem 'The Twofold Tree' translates a passage from Book VI of Virgil's *Aeneid*. The dedication for this poem and for the book as a whole is to my father, Dennis William West (1940-2015).

Once again I would like to extend my gratitude to Magica Fossati, Oliver Dennis and David Musgrave for their encouragement and editorial assistance. My thanks go also to the Literature Board of The Australia Council for the Arts, and to the editors of the following publications where some poems first appeared: *Antipodes*, *LEA Lingue e letterature d'Oriente e d'Occidente*, *Poetry Ireland Review*, *Sydney Review of Books*, and *The Weekend Australian*.